# Knotted Jewelry

## Make It! • Wear It! • Love It!

KALMBACH BOOKS

WAUKESHA, WI

**Kalmbach Books**
21027 Crossroads Circle
Waukesha, Wisconsin 53186
www.JewelryAndBeadingStore.com

Step-by-step photos by the authors. All other photography © 2015 Kalmbach Books except where otherwise noted.

Published in 2015
19 18 17 16 15    1 2 3 4 5

Manufactured in the China.

ISBN: 978-1-62700-332-2
EISBN: 978-1-62700-333-9

The material in this book has appeared previously in *Bead&Button* and *Bead Style* magazines. *Bead&Button* and *BeadStyle* are registered as trademarks.

**Editor:** Dianne Wheeler
**Book Design:** Lisa Bergman

# CONTENTS

## Beads & pendants

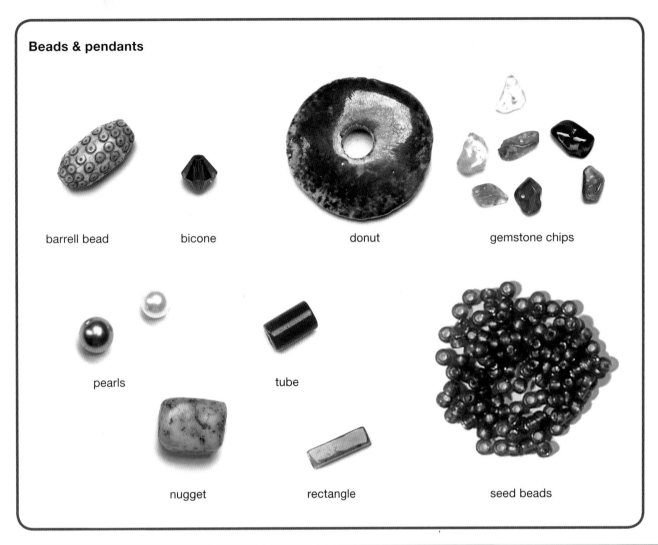

barrell bead

bicone

donut

gemstone chips

pearls

tube

nugget

rectangle

seed beads

## Findings

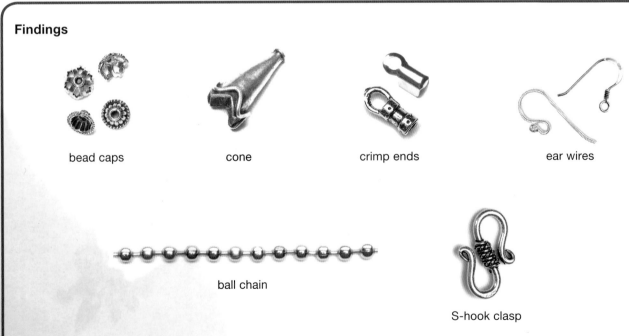

bead caps

cone

crimp ends

ear wires

ball chain

S-hook clasp

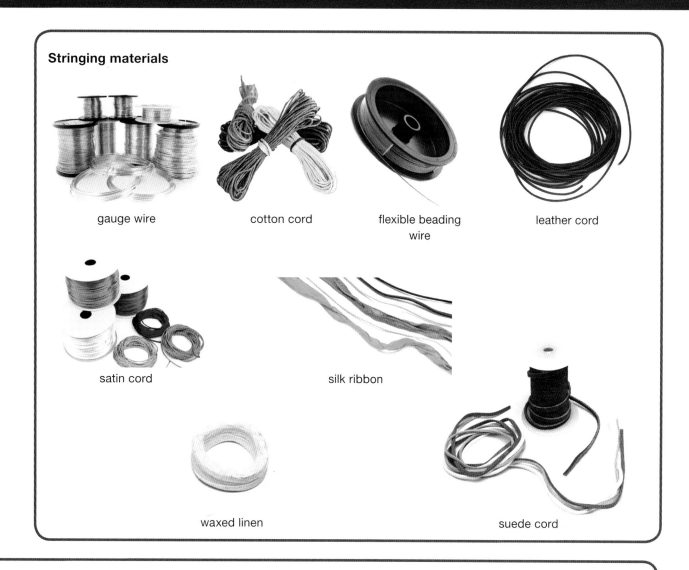

## Stringing materials

gauge wire

cotton cord

flexible beading
wire

leather cord

satin cord

silk ribbon

waxed linen

suede cord

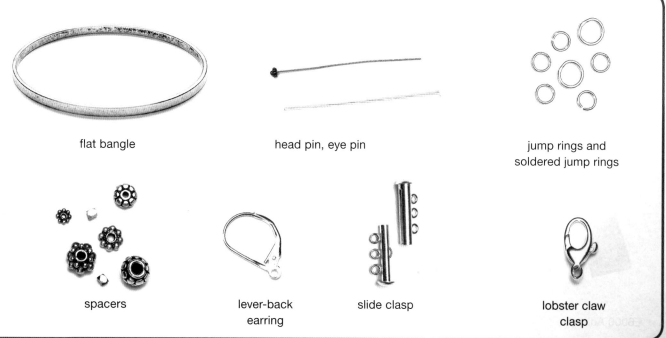

flat bangle

head pin, eye pin

jump rings and
soldered jump rings

spacers

lever-back
earring

slide clasp

lobster claw
clasp

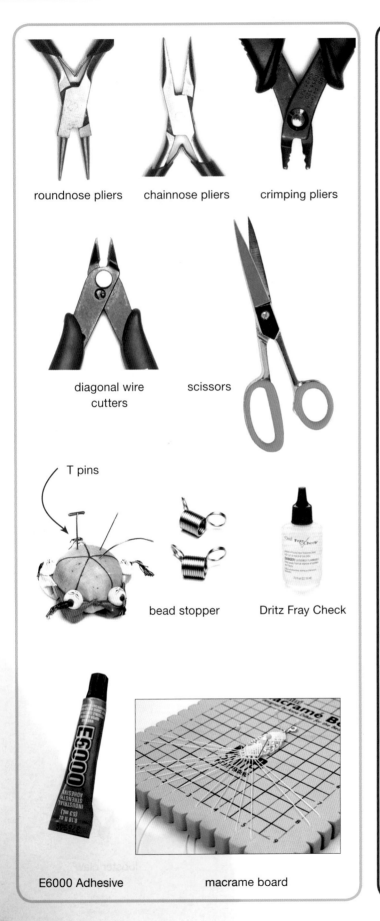

roundnose pliers    chainnose pliers    crimping pliers

diagonal wire
cutters    scissors

T pins

bead stopper    Dritz Fray Check

E6000 Adhesive    macrame board

## Overhand knot

Make a loop with the
thread. Pull the tail
through the loop, and
tighten.

## Square knot

**1** Cross one end of
the thread over and
under the other end.
Pull both ends to
tighten the first half
of the knot.

**2** Cross the first end
of the thread over
and under the other
end. Pull both ends
to tighten the knot.

## Surgeon's knot

**1** Cross one end of the
thread over and under the
other twice. Pull both ends
to tighten the first half of
the knot.
**2** Cross the first end of the
thread over and under the
other end. Pull both ends to
tighten the knot.

## Macramé square knot

**1** Cross the right-hand cord over the core and
the left-hand cord under the core. This creates a
loop between each cord and the core. Pass the
right-hand cord through the loop on the left from
front to back and the left-hand cord through the
other loop from back to front **(left)**.
**2** Cross the left-hand cord over and the right-
hand cord under the core. Pass the cords
through the loops **(right),** and tighten.

## Stringing & wirework

### Crimping

Use crimp beads to secure flexible beading wire. Slide the crimp bead into place, and

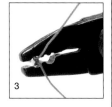

squeeze it firmly with chainnose pliers to flatten it. For a more finished look, use crimping pliers:

**1** Position the crimp bead in the hole that is closest to the handle of the crimping pliers.

**2** Holding the wires apart, squeeze the pliers to compress the crimp bead, making sure one wire is on each side of the dent.

**3** Place the crimp bead in the front hole of the pliers, and position it so the dent is facing the tips of the pliers. Squeeze the pliers to fold the crimp in half.

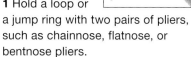

### Opening and closing loops and jump rings

**1** Hold a loop or a jump ring with two pairs of pliers, such as chainnose, flatnose, or bentnose pliers.

**2** To open the loop or jump ring, bring the tips of one pair of pliers toward you, and push the tips of the other pair away from you.

**3** The open jump ring. Reverse the steps to close.

### Plain loop

**1** ]Using chainnose pliers, make a right-angle bend in the wire directly above a bead or other component or at least 1/4 in. (6 mm) from the end of a naked piece of wire. For a larger loop, bend the wire further in.

**2** Grip the end of the wire with roundnose pliers so that the wire is flush with the jaws of the pliers where they meet. The closer to the tip of the pliers that you work, the smaller the loop will be. Press downward slightly, and rotate the wire toward the bend made in step 1.

**3** Reposition the pliers in the loop to continue rotating the wire until the end of the wire touches the bend.

**4** The plain loop.

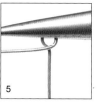 

### Wrapped loop

**1** Using chain-nose pliers, make a right-angle bend in the wire about 2 mm above a bead or other component or at least 1¼ in. (3.2 cm) from the end of a naked piece of wire.

**2** Position the jaws of the roundnose pliers in the bend. The closer to the tip of the pliers that you work, the smaller the loop will be.

**3** Curve the short end of the wire over the top jaw of the roundnose pliers.

**4** Reposition the pliers so the lower jaw fits snugly in the loop. Curve the wire downward around the bottom jaw of the pliers. This is the first half of a wrapped loop.

**5** To complete the wraps, grasp the top of the loop with one pair of pliers.

**6** With another pair of pliers, wrap the wire around the stem two or three times. Trim the excess wire, and gently press the cut end close to the wraps with chainnose pliers.

# Projects

Attach bubbly beads to
bright cotton cord

designed by Ashley Bunting

# Knotted Lucite
## necklace

Lucite beads — drops, disks, rounds, and saucers — are available in fun finishes,
so mix them up in one standout necklace. Find cotton cord to suit your style: Go
with a neutral for versatility or a contrasting bright for a pop of color. Then tie it all
together with one basic knot.

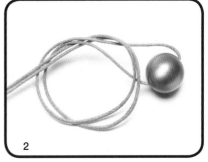

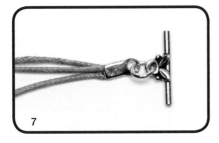

**1** necklace • Cut a 5–6-ft. (1.5–1.8 m) piece of waxed cotton cord. Make a "needle" (p.11) and string 13 to 19 beads on the cord. Tape the ends or use Bead Stoppers.

**2** On the center of the cord, with the center bead, tie an overhand knot (Basics, p. 6).

**3** Pull the ends of the cord to tighten the knot.

**4** On each side, with the next bead, tie an overhand knot about 1 in. (2.5 cm) from the center knot.

**5** On each side, with the next bead, tie an overhand knot about 1 in. (2.5 cm) from the previous knot. Repeat until the strand is within 1 in. (2.5 cm) of the finished length. Make three beaded strands.

**6** Gather the three strands, leaving at least ½ in. (1.3 cm) of cord on each end. Trim the excess cord. On each side, over all three ends, use chainnose pliers to attach a crimp end.

**7** On each end, open a jump ring (Basics). Attach half of a clasp and close the jump ring.

## "The finished pieces are fun, colorful, and lightweight!"

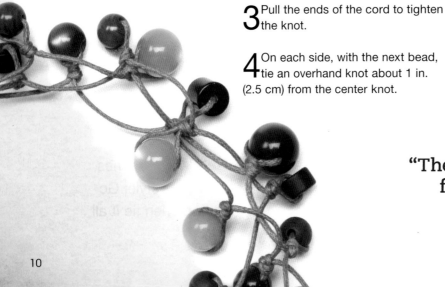

**1**

**2**

**3**

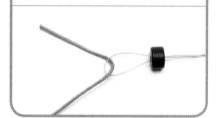

## Make a "needle"

For easier stringing: Cut a 4-in. (10 cm) piece of .014 or .015 beading wire and fold it in half to make a loop. Thread the cord's tail through the loop, and pull the ends of the "needle" through the bead.

## Materials

**necklace 16–21 in. (41–53 cm)**

- ◆ 39–57 6–13 mm Lucite beads
- ◆ 15–18 ft. (4.6–5.25 m) waxed cotton cord, 1 mm diameter
- ◆ flexible beading wire, .014 or .015
- ◆ 2 4–5 mm jump rings
- ◆ 2 crimp ends
- ◆ clasp
- ◆ 2 Bead Stoppers (optional)
- ◆ chainnose and roundnose pliers
- ◆ diagonal wire cutters

**earrings**

- ◆ 6 6–13 mm Lucite beads
- ◆ 1 in. (2.5 cm) chain, 3 mm links
- ◆ 6 1½-in. (3.8 cm) head pins
- ◆ pair of earring wires
- ◆ chainnose and roundnose pliers
- ◆ diagonal wire cutters

**1** earrings • For each earring: On a head pin, string a bead. Make a plain loop (Basics). Make three bead units.

**2** Cut a five-link piece of chain. Open the loop of each bead unit (Basics). Attach a bead unit to the center link and to each end link, closing the loops as you go.

**3** Open the loop of an earring wire. Attach the dangle and close the loop.

# Knot your average
## pearl necklace

**Use two styles of knots to accent large-hole pearls strung on leather cord**

designed by Ayla Phillips Pizzo

You'll be surprised at how easy it is to tie beautiful (and intentional!) knots with 1.5 mm round leather cord. Coiled knots take on the look of accent beads while simple overhand knots are the perfect stoppers for pretty pearls.

### Toggle loop

**1** Cut a 21-in. (53 cm) piece of leather cord, and make a bend 6½ in. (16.5 cm) from one end. Pinch the doubled cord to form a loop **(photo a)**.

**2** Loosely coil the short end around the doubled cord three or four times, coiling toward the loop **(photo b)**. Feed the short end back through the coil, and tighten the coil by pulling on the loop and the short end **(photo c)**.

**3** Test the size of the loop with a 10 mm pearl, which will serve as the toggle bead. The pearl and a small knot must be able to pass snugly through the loop. To make the loop bigger, pull on the loop.

To make the loop smaller, pull on the short end.

**4** Trim the short end close to the coil. Apply glue to the coil. Let dry for two to three minutes.

### Center pearl

**1** Make a bend in the cord 7½ in. (19.1 cm) from the other end, and pinch the doubled cord to form a very small (4–6 mm) loop.

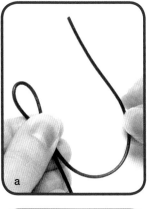

## Materials

**necklace**

**17–18 in. (43–46 cm)***

◆ 5 10 mm large-hole pearls (maroon)
◆ 1½ yd. (1.4 m) 1.5 mm leather cord (black)
◆ Super New Glue
◆ wire cutters

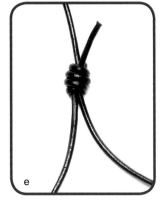

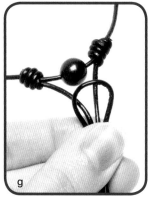

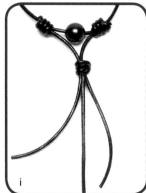

**2** Loosely coil the short end around the long end three or four times, coiling away from the loop **(photo d)**. Feed the short end back through the coil, but do not tighten the coil.

**3** Cut a 3-in. (7.6 cm) piece of cord, and feed one end into the coil. Tighten the coil by pulling on the short end, causing the loop to disappear and become part of the coil **(photo e)**. Make sure that there is about 7½ in. (19.1 cm) of cord between the toggle loop coil and the coil just made. String a pearl on the 3-in. (7.6 cm) cord.

**4** Cut a 21-in. (53 cm) piece of cord, and make a bend 6½ in. (16.5 cm) from one end. Work as in step 2 to create a loose coil. Holding the

pearl in place, feed the other end of the 3-in. (7.6 cm) cord into the coil. Tighten the coil. Trim the 3-in. (7.6 cm) cord close to the coils **(photo f)**, apply glue to both coils. Let dry.

### Pearl dangles

**1** Cut a 9-in. (23 cm) piece of cord, fold it in half, and hold it against the two cords that extend below the center pearl **(photo g)**.

**2** With one half of the 9-in. (23 cm) cord, loosely coil around the other three cords three or four times, coiling away from the fold **(photo h)**. Feed the short end back through the coil, and tighten the coil. Trim the short end close to the coil **(photo i)**, apply glue to the coil, and let dry.

**3** You should now have three cords that extend below the center pearl. On one cord, string a pearl, and tie an overhand knot (Basics) below it. Repeat with the remaining cords, adjusting the knots so that the pearls hang at the desired lengths. Trim any excess cord below the knots, apply glue to the knots, and let dry.

### Toggle bead

**1** On the remaining cord opposite the toggle loop, string a pearl. Tie an overhand knot above the pearl so that the pearl will line up with the toggle loop. Trim any excess cord.

**2** Slide the pearl down the cord, and apply glue to where the pearl was positioned previously. Slide the pearl back in place. Apply glue to the knot as well, and let dry.

# Embellish a bangle

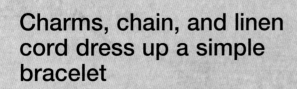

## Charms, chain, and linen cord dress up a simple bracelet

### designed by Lorelei Eurto

I was inspired by the popular designs that incorporate the technique of wrapping waxed linen cord around ball chain in a long wrap-style bracelet. I thought the technique would look equally cool on a bangle, adding a bit of extra texture. With a couple of hole punches and some wire, I attached a metal embellishment as a focal point; charms dangling from jump rings add to the eclectic effect.

## Materials

**bangle**

- ◆ 27 mm metal embellishment
- ◆ 16–22 mm charm or metal embellishment
- ◆ 17–20 mm flower bead, center drilled
- ◆ 12 mm flower bead, center drilled
- ◆ 3 mm round spacer
- ◆ 12 mm bead cap
- ◆ 6 in. (15 cm) 22-gauge wire
- ◆ 42 in. (1.2 m) waxed linen cord, 4 ply
- ◆ 10 in. (25 cm) ball chain, 2.4 mm
- ◆ flat bangle
- ◆ 2-in. (5 cm) head pin
- ◆ **2** 10 mm jump rings
- ◆ chainnose and roundnose pliers
- ◆ hole-punch pliers
- ◆ diagonal wire cutters
- ◆ two-hole punch (optional)
- ◆ glue such as Super New Glue (optional)

**1** In the center of a metal embellishment, make two marks about ¼ in. (6 mm) apart.

**2** Use hole-punch pliers to punch a hole at each mark.

**3** Cut a 6-in. (15 cm) piece of wire. String the embellishment on the wire and center it on a bangle. Wrap the wire around the bangle to secure the embellishment. Trim the excess wire and use chainnose pliers to tuck the ends.

**4** Cut a 42-in. (1.2 m) piece of waxed linen cord. Leaving a ½-in. (1.3 cm) tail, tie an overhand knot (Basics, p. 6) around the bangle next to the embellishment.

**5** Cut a piece of ball chain long enough to cover the rest of the bangle. Set the end of the ball chain over the knotted cord, and wrap the working end of the cord around the bangle and in the space between the first and second balls. Continue wrapping between each ball, covering the tail as you go. Pull the cord tight as you complete each wrap to ensure even tension.

**6** In the last space in the ball chain, wrap the cord and tie an overhand knot. Wrap and tie additional knots to secure the cord. Trim the excess cord close to the knots. If desired, apply glue to the knots.

**7** On a head pin, string a spacer, two flower beads, and a bead cap. Make a wrapped loop (Basics).

**8** Open a jump ring (Basics). Attach the bead unit and the bangle and close the jump ring. Use jump rings to attach charms or embellishments as desired.

# Tied to turquoise

Whip up a necklace and earrings with turquoise and knotted cord

designed by Irina Miech

With so many cord colors and varieties of turquoise, it's easy to choose a combination that you feel attached to. Try bright blue turquoise and matching cord for sweet femininity. Or pair green gems and black cord for earthy sophistication. Without a clasp, this lengthy necklace slips easily over your head. Simple nugget earrings set your look in stone.

**1** necklace • Tie an overhand knot (Basics, p. 6) 4 in. (10 cm) from the end of a beading cord. String: 4 mm spacer, 6 mm round bead, 9 mm spacer, round, 4 mm spacer. Tie an overhand knot.

**2** Tie an overhand knot 1 in. (2.5 cm) from the previous knot. String three to five gemstone chips and tie an overhand knot.

**3** Tie an overhand knot 1 in. (2.5 cm) from the previous knot. String a 4 mm spacer, a nugget, and a 4 mm spacer. Tie an overhand knot.

**4** Repeat the patterns in steps 1 to 3 (or string new patterns) until the necklace is within 4 in. (10 cm) of the finished length.

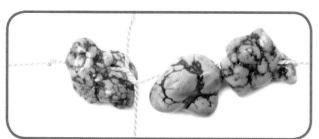

**5** Tie an overhand knot 1 in. (2.5 cm) from the previous knot. String nuggets as desired. Tie a surgeon's knot (Basics). Trim the ends and glue the knot.

**tip**

To tie a knot close to a bead: Use roundnose pliers to grasp the cord next to the bead. Tie a knot by looping the cord around the pliers' tip. As you tighten the knot, slide the pliers out.

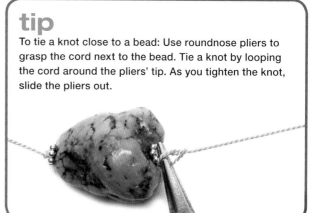

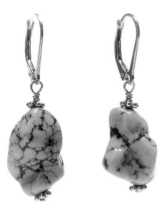

**1** earrings • On a head pin, string a spacer, a nugget, and a spacer. Make a wrapped loop (Basics).

**2** Open the loop of an earring wire (Basics) and attach the dangle. Close the loop. Make a second earring to match the first.

## Materials

**necklace (blue 21 in./53 cm)**
- ◆ **4–6** 18–22 mm nuggets
- ◆ 16-in. (41 cm) strand 8–12 mm gemstone chips
- ◆ **12–16** 6 mm round beads)
- ◆ **7–9** 9 mm spacers, in two styles
- ◆ **16–20** 4 mm spacers
- ◆ silk beading cord, size 4
- ◆ roundnose pliers
- ◆ diagonal wire cutters
- ◆ G-S Hypo Cement

**earrings**
- ◆ **2** 18–22 mm nuggets)
- ◆ **4** 4 mm spacers
- ◆ **2** 2-in. (5 cm) head pins
- ◆ pair of lever-back earring wires
- ◆ chainnose and roundnose pliers
- ◆ diagonal wire cutters

## design alternative

Instead of tying knots, string bead bumpers. Then move beads along the beading cord.

> **❝** Working with turquoise always makes me think of Santa Fe and the timeless beauty of its landscape and people.**❞**

# Knotted donut *necklace*

String graduated focal
beads on leather cord for
a seaside statement

designed by Kelly Conedera

The gorgeous African island of Seychelles inspired this eclectic turquoise necklace. Summery and earthy, it reflects the island vibe with a sea-and-sand palette. Or try it in black — it's the perfect accessory for a long tank dress while you're lounging poolside.

1 Cut a 3-ft. (.9 m) piece of leather cord. Fold the cord in half and thread it through the center of a 50 mm donut. Thread both ends through the fold and tighten the cord.

2 Over both cord ends, string a 35–40 mm barrel bead. Tie a Chinese button knot, treating both cords as one (p. 21).

3 On one end, string a tube bead, leaving ½ in. (1.3 cm) of cord below the Chinese knot. String a spacer and an oxyhedron bead. Tie a Chinese button knot. Trim the cord 1 in. (2.5 cm) below the knot. Repeat on the remaining cord, leaving 1 in. (2.5 cm) between the first Chinese knot and the tube bead.

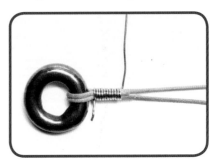

4 Cut two 3-ft. (.9 m) pieces of cord. On one end, over both cords, string a 20–24 mm ring, leaving a ¾-in. (1.9 cm) tail. Cut a 10-in. (25 cm) piece of wire. Using chainnose pliers, on one end of the wire make a hook. Hook it around the cords below the ring. Wrap the wire around the cords to secure, extending beyond the cord ends. Trim and tuck the excess wire.

5 Treating both cords as one, tie a Chinese button knot. Over the ends of both cords, string two 10–12 mm large-hole metal beads.

6 Separate the cords. With one cord, go over and under a 30–35 mm donut. With the other cord, go under and over to weave through the donut. Over both ends, string a nugget or two 14–16 mm large-hole beads.

7 Repeat step 6, weaving around a 40 mm donut, the 50 mm donut from step 1, another 40 mm donut, and a 30–35 mm donut. Omit the last nugget or large-hole beads.

**8** String two 10–12 mm large-hole metal beads. Treating both cords as one, tie a Chinese button knot.

**9** Trim the cords to 1½ in. (3.8 cm). String a 20–24 mm ring and fold the ends over it. Secure the ends as in step 4.

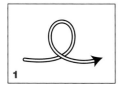
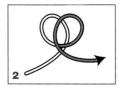

**10** Cut a 2-in. (5 cm) and a 5-in. (13 cm) piece of 19–20 mm link chain. On each end of the necklace, open an end link of chain (Basics) and attach the ring. Close the link. On the remaining end link of the short chain, use a jump ring to attach a lobster claw clasp.

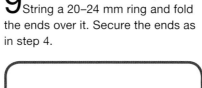

**11** Use a jump ring to attach a charm to the end link of 5-in. (13 cm) chain.

## Materials

**necklace 18–20 in. (46–51 cm)**

- ◆ 50 mm donut
- ◆ **2** 44 mm donuts
- ◆ **2** 30–35 mm donuts
- ◆ **2** 20–24 mm rings
- ◆ 35–40 mm barrel bead
- ◆ **2** 25 mm tube beads
- ◆ **4** 16–20 mm large-hole nuggets or **8** 14–16 mm large-hole beads
- ◆ **6** 10–12 mm large-hole metal beads
- ◆ **2** 10–12 mm oxyhedron or bicone beads
- ◆ 15 mm charm
- ◆ 3 yds. (2.7 m) leather cord, 1.5 or 2 mm diameter
- ◆ 7 in. (18 cm) chain, 19–20 mm links
- ◆ 20 in. (51 cm) 18- or 20-gauge wire
- ◆ **2** 10 mm jump rings
- ◆ lobster claw clasp
- ◆ **2** pairs of chainnose pliers
- ◆ diagonal wire cutters

# Chinese button knots

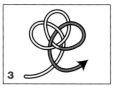

**1** Make a counterclockwise loop in the cord and hold the bottom of the loop with your left thumb and forefinger.

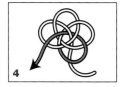

**2** Make a second counter-clockwise loop overlapping the first loop.

**3** Make a third counterclockwise loop, bringing the cord end down through the loop on the right, up through the middle section, and down and under the left loop. Bring the end over the fixed end.

**4** Bring the end down through the right loop, under the next two cords, up through the center area, and across the remaining cords.

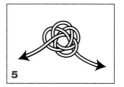

**5** Gently and slowly pull the ends in opposite directions. The shape of the knot will begin to form.

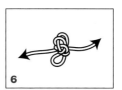

**6** Pull the knot to start tightening it. A loop or two will stick out.

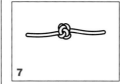

**7** Move the knot into position by holding the cord that is on the side you want to move the knot toward, and pushing the cord into the knot. Note which loop is linked to the cord you pushed. Pull that loop until the knot is in the desired position. **Continue pulling loop by loop to take up slack, turning the knot in the same direction and tightening through each loop until the knot is snug.**

# Pearl vine bracelet

## Knot your way to a casual, adjustable accessory.

### designed by Ayla Phillips Pizzo

## Toggle loop

**1** Cut four 18-in. (46 cm) pieces of 1 mm leather cord, and keep them nearby.

**2** Cut a 10-in. (25 cm) piece of 1.5 mm leather cord, and make a bend 7 in. (18 cm) from one end. Pinch the doubled cord to form a loop **(photo a)**.

**3** Loosely coil the longer end around the doubled cord three or four times, coiling toward the loop **(photo b)**. Feed the long end back through the coil. Insert the ends of the four 1 mm cords into the coil so that they are parallel with the long end of the 1.5 mm cord. Tighten the coil by pulling on the loop and the long end **(photo c)**.

**4** Test the size of the loop with an 8 mm pearl, which will serve as a toggle pearl. The pearl and a small knot must be able to pass snugly through the loop. To make the loop bigger, pull on

the loop. To make the loop smaller, pull on the long end of the 1.5 mm cord.

**5** Trim both ends of the 1.5 mm cord and the short ends of the 1 mm cords close to the coil. You should now have four cords exiting the coil **(photo d)**. Apply glue to the coil, and let dry for two to three minutes.

## Center pearls

**1** On your work surface, arrange the four cords so they are parallel. On an outer cord, string a pearl, and slide it close to the coil. Bring the four cords together after the pearl, and tie an overhand knot (Basics, p. 6) with all of the cords, keeping them parallel and in order **(photo e)**. Aim to tie the knot no more than ¾ in. (1.9 cm) from the coil.

**2** On each outer cord, string a pearl, and slide them close to the previous knot. Bring the four cords together after the pearls, and tie another overhand

knot about ¾ in. (1.9 cm) from the previous knot **(photo f)**.

**3** Repeat steps 1 and 2 until you have seven pearl sections. For the repeats of step 1, string the pearl on alternating outer cords.

## Toggle pearls

**1** On two cords, string a pearl, and tie an overhand knot after the pearl at the desired "first length" for your adjustable bracelet **(photo g)**. On the remaining two cords, string a pearl, and tie an overhand knot at the desired second length. Trim the ends close to both knots. Apply glue to the knots, and let dry.

**2** Slide the toggle pearls away from the end knots, apply glue to the cords where the pearls were previously, and slide the pearls back over the glue. Let dry.

## Materials

**bracelet 6½–8 in. (16.5–20 cm)**

◆ **12** 8 mm large-hole pearls (cream)
◆ 10 in. (25 cm) 1.5 mm leather cord (black)
◆ 2 yd. (1.8 m) 1 mm leather cord (black)
◆ Super New Glue
◆ wire cutters

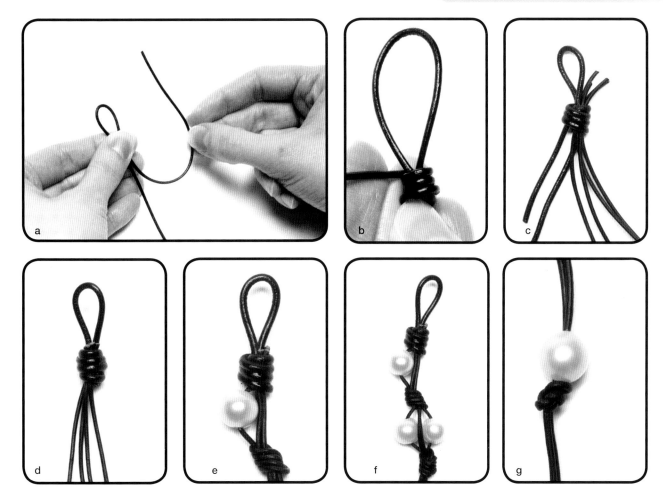

# CLASP options:

This double-toggle closure allows you to wear your bracelet at two different lengths! Slide both toggle pearls into the loop for the shorter version, or single out the longest pearl for more length.

# Coined at the hip

### designed by Jane Konkel

This chic belt will display a cache of Chinese-replica coins, beach stones, and gemstone donuts securely on your hip. The coins are tied with snake knots — fitting because the snake is one of the 12 animals of the Chinese zodiac and is thought to be the guardian of treasure.

## Materials
- **3–5** 38mm coins, center drilled
- **2–4** beach-stone donuts
- **6–8** 20–30mm gemstone donuts, in two sizes
- **14–16** 15–20mm single-loop coins, in two sizes
- **14–18** 5mm inside diameter antique-gold jump rings
- **9–11** ft. (2.7–3.4m) 2mm woven cord
- chainnose and roundnose pliers or **2** pairs of chainnose pliers
- diagonal wire cutters

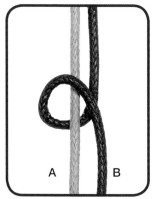

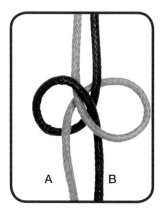

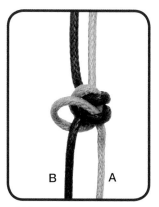

**1** **a** Determine the finished length of your belt. (Mine is 60 in./1.5m.) Multiply that number by 3, and cut two pieces of cord to that length. Center a 38mm coin on one cord.

**b** To tie a snake knot: String cord B under and over cord A, making a loop.

**2** String A over B and through the first loop, making a loop with A. Pull both ends to loosely close the knot.

**3** String B under A and down through A's loop. Pull B to loosely close the knot.

**4** Turn the cords over. String A under B and down through the lower of the two loops. Pull cord A to loosely close the knot.

**5** Turn the cords over. Approximately 1 in. (2.5cm) from the knot, tie a snake knot. String a donut, crossing each end through the center.

Tie a snake knot.

**6** Continue stringing donuts and 38mm coins and tying snake knots until the knotted section is within 2 in. (5cm) of half the desired length.

Approximately 1 in. (2.5cm) from the last knot, tie a snake knot. Turn the cords over, and repeat steps 3 and 4 four times. String a 38mm coin.

**7** Tie a snake knot. Turn the cords over, and repeat steps 3 and 4 four times.

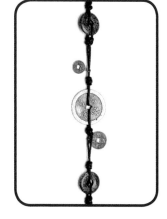

**8** Open a jump ring (Basics, p. 6) and attach a single-loop coin. Close the jump ring. On the end of one cord, string the coin, leaving a 2-in. (5cm) tail. Tie an overhand knot (Basics). Trim the excess cord. Repeat with the remaining cord.

**9** To finish the other half of the belt: Center the 38mm coin (from step 1) on the second cord. Repeat steps 1b–8. Use jump rings to attach single-loop coins to the cord between knots.

## tips
• To distinguish cord A from cord B, the photos in steps 1–4 show cords in different colors.
• Learn how to tie a snake knot and other decorative Chinese knots in Suzen Millodot's.

You can wear the slide in the front or the back of the necklace.

# Lariat
## with slide
## clasp

designed by Linda Osterhoudt

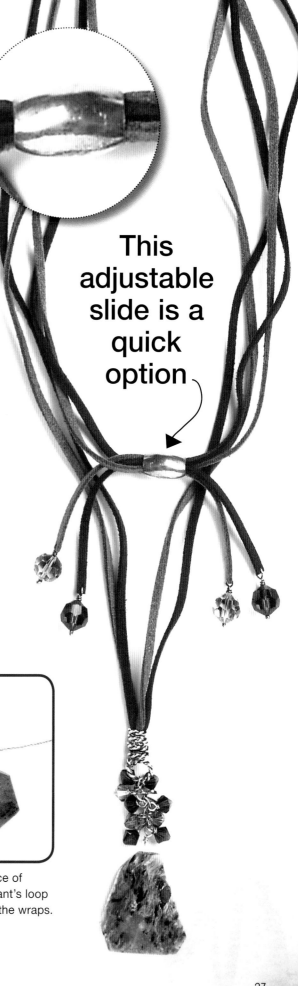

This adjustable slide is a quick option

A large-hole bead can be a clever substitute for a clasp on a suede lariat. This version features long cords in two colors and a bail wrapped with twisted wire. Crystals dress up this otherwise organic piece.

**1** On a 2½-in. (6.4cm) head pin, string a pendant. (If the pendant's hole is large, string a spacer first.) Make the first half of a wrapped loop (Basics, p. 7).

**2** Cut a ¾-in. (1.9cm) piece of chain. Attach the pendant's loop to the chain and complete the wraps.

**3** On a 1½-in. (3.8cm) head pin, string a crystal. Make the first half of a wrapped loop. Repeat with the remaining crystals. Set the round-crystal units aside for step 9.

**4** Attach two bicone-crystal units to each link and complete the wraps.

**5** Cut a 10-in. (25cm) piece of twisted wire. Make the first half of a wrapped loop. Attach the dangle and complete the wraps.

**6** Decide how long you want your lariat to be. (My lariats are 44 in./1.1m.) Cut two pieces of suede cord to that length.

Cut a 4-in. (10cm) piece of 20-gauge wire. Make a wrapped loop. Center the loop over both cords. Fold the cords in half and wrap the wire around both cords. Trim the excess wire.

**7** Wrap the twisted wire around the 20-gauge wire wraps. Trim the excess wire and tuck the wire tail.

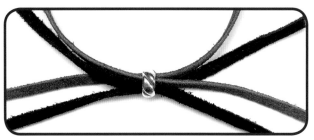

**8** String each pair of cords through a large-hole bead in opposite directions. Check the fit, and trim the cords if necessary.

**9** Using a thumbtack, pierce a hole approximately ⅛ in. (3mm) from each end of each cord. String a round-crystal unit through each pierced hole, and complete the wraps.

## Materials

**gemstone pendant, approximately 30mm**

- ◆ **4** 8mm round crystals, in two colors
- ◆ **10–14** 6mm bicone crystals, in two colors
- ◆ large-hole metal bead
- ◆ 4mm spacer (optional)
- ◆ **2** 40–48-in. (1–1.2m) pieces 3mm suede cord
- ◆ 4 in. (10cm) 20-gauge half-hard wire
- ◆ 10 in. (25cm) 18- or 20-gauge twisted wire
- ◆ ¾ in. (1.9cm) chain, 3–4mm links
- ◆ 2½-in. (6.4cm) head pin or decorative head pin
- ◆ **14–18** 1½-in. (3.8cm) head pins or decorative head pins
- ◆ chainnose and roundnose pliers
- ◆ diagonal wire cutters
- ◆ thumbtack

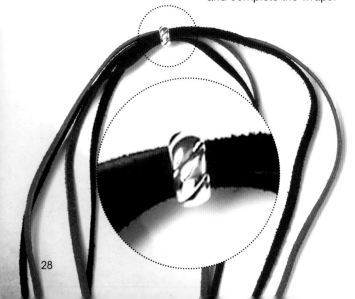

# Nothing
## if ... knot
# versatile

# designed by Linda Jones

This necklace can be created with cotton cord, ribbon, leather, or suede. It can be lengthened for a belt or shortened for a bracelet. The hook clasp can fasten anywhere, with the bead tassel in front or back.

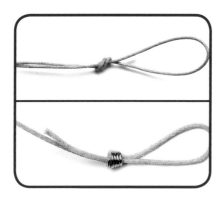

**1** Determine the finished length of your necklace. (The green necklace is 16 in./41cm; the black necklace, 24 in./61cm.) Triple the number and cut a piece of cord to that length.

Fold the cord, leaving a ¾-in. (1.9cm) loop. Tie an overhand knot (Basics, p. 104). Glue the knot. Cut a 3-in. (7.6cm) piece of wire. Tightly coil it around the knot. Trim the excess cord.

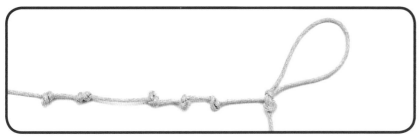

**2** Make a series of overhand knots along the cord in sets of twos and threes. Make sure the knots are big enough to act as stoppers for the jump rings. If necessary, make two knots at each point.

Repeat until the strand is within 3 in. (7.6cm) of the desired length. Check the fit, allowing 1 in. (2.5cm) for the clasp. Tie an overhand knot and make a coil around it as in step 1.

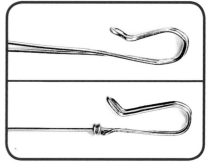

**3a** Cut a 4-in. (10cm) piece of wire. Fold it in half. Using roundnose pliers, bend the wire into a hook.

**b** Wrap one wire around the other near the base of the hook. Trim the excess wrapping wire.

**4** String three beads on the wire stem and make a plain loop (Basics) on the stem next to the last bead.

Open the loop and attach one end of the cord. Close the loop.

**5** Determine the total number of dangles. You'll need one or two fewer dangles than the number of knots, plus eight for the tassel.

Make about one-third of the dangles with coil ends. For each, cut a 3-in. (7.6cm) piece of wire and make a small coil on one end with roundnose pliers. String an 8º or 11º seed bead and a glass bead. Make a wrapped loop (Basics) above the top bead.

**6** Make one-third of the dangles with loop ends. For each, cut a 3-in. (7.6cm) piece of wire and make a small loop at one end with roundnose pliers. String an 8º or 11º and a glass bead. Make a wrapped loop above the top bead.

**7** Make one-third of the dangles with decorative wire wraps. For each, cut a 4-in. (10cm) piece of wire. Bend it in half and string a glass bead. Wrap one wire end around the bead. Make a set of wraps above the bead.

Make a wrapped loop above the wraps. Trim the excess wire.

**8** To make a coil dangle, cut a 1½-in. (3.8cm) piece of wire and make a loop on one end. String 1 in. (2.5cm) of 8°s or 11°s. Make a loop above the top bead.

Using your fingers, shape the bead unit into a coil.

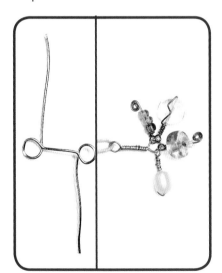

**9** **a** Cut a 3-in. (7.6cm) piece of wire. Leaving ½ in. (1.3cm) of wire in the center, make the first half of a wrapped loop on each end.

**b** Attach the remaining cord loop to one end and four dangles to the other. Complete the wraps.

**10** Open a jump ring (Basics). Attach two dangles and the wrapped-loop end. Close the jump ring. Use jump rings to attach several dangles as desired.

## Materials

- ◆ **24–40** 6–20mm glass beads in assorted shapes
- ◆ 2g 8° or 11° seed beads
- ◆ 4–6 ft. (1.2–1.8m) cotton cord
- ◆ 8–12 ft. (2.4–3.7m) 24-gauge half-hard wire
- ◆ **4** 5–8mm jump rings
- ◆ **16–32** 5mm jump rings
- ◆ chainnose and roundnose pliers
- ◆ diagonal wire cutters
- ◆ E6000 adhesive

**11** Using a jump ring, attach a dangle to the cord between the end loop and the first knot. Close the jump ring. Using jump rings, attach one or two dangles between each knot.

Tie a water-themed charm to your rope bracelet with bright thread.

# Sail
## away

## Make a continuous Turk's head knot with one long cord

designed by
Jane Konkel

Back in the day, a sailor would make bracelets from the extra ropes on his ship and give them to a loved one to wear for good luck while he was at sea. I'm making one for each of the swim instructors at my neighborhood pool. Make a few this summer as tokens of friendship, good luck, or connectedness, or just to proclaim your love for the water.

1 Cut a 9-ft. (2.7 m) piece of macramé cord. Apply glue to the working end to stiffen it. Tape the other end to the left side of a cylindrical object. Make one wrap, crossing the cords to make an X (point A).

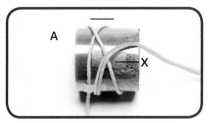

2 Make another wrap, bringing the working cord between the two fixed cords and crossing over the right cord to form another X (Tape trick, p. 33). Tape the X.

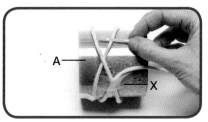

3 Above point A, string the working cord under the cord on the right.

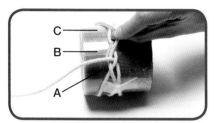

**4** Cross the left fixed cord over the right. Note the new crossings at points B and C.

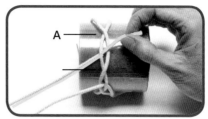

**5** Between B and C, string the working cord under the left cord and over the right cord.

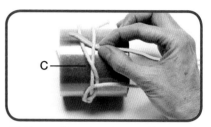

**6** Above C, string the working cord under the right cord.

**7** Cross the left fixed cord over the right as in step 4.

**8** String the working cord under the left cord and over the right cord as in step 5.

**9** Above the X, string the working cord under the right cord, then over the left cord as in step 6. Repeat steps 4, 5, and 6 until you reach the starting point. Remove the tape from step 2.

## tape trick
Allow some slack when taping in step 2. You will need to double the plait, then triple it.

**10** String the working cord following the path in steps 1 to 9 to double the plait. Continue until you reach the starting point.

**11** Remove the bracelet from the cylinder. String the working cord through again, following the path to triple the plait.

**12** String the ends to the inside of the bracelet. Trim the ends to ½ in. (1.3 cm).

**13** If desired, use a lighter to seal the ends. Glue each end to the inside of the bracelet.

## Materials
- 9 ft. (2.7 m) 2–3 mm macramé cord
- bracelet mandrel or other cylindrical object, 2¾ in. (7 cm) or 3 in. (7.6 cm) diameter
- Super New Glue
- scissors
- lighter (optional)

# Six silky strands

## Tie knots to make a lightweight silk necklace

**designed by Michelle Mach**

Punctuate strands of colorful cord with black or white beads. Skip the ruler on this one; just space five or six beads on each strand, and secure them with overhand knots.

## Materials

**necklace 27 in. (69 cm)**

- ◆ **30–50** 9 mm large-hole beads
- ◆ **12** 7 mm large-hole beads or spacers
- ◆ **6** 42-in. (1.1 m) silk cords, in different colors
- ◆ **2** ft. (61 cm) 26-gauge half-hard wire
- ◆ six-strand slide clasp
- ◆ chainnose and crimping pliers
- ◆ diagonal wire cutters

**1** On one silk cord, string a 9 mm bead. Tie an overhand knot (Basics, p. 6) on each side of the bead.

**2** On each side, a few inches from the previous knot, tie a knot. String a bead and tie a knot. Repeat, stringing five or six beads on the cord.

**3** String beads and tie knots on the remaining cords. Vary the length between the knots on each cord, leaving approximately 1–4 in. (2.5–10 cm) between knots.

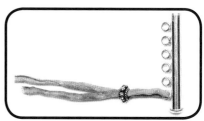

**4** On each end of one cord, string a 7 mm bead or spacer and the corresponding loop of the clasp. Go back through the bead, leaving a 2-in. (5 cm) tail. Check the fit, and trim cord if necessary.

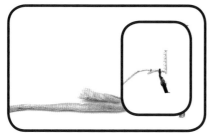

**5** Cut a 2-in. (5 cm) piece of wire. Use chainnose pliers to wrap the wire tightly around the gathered cords. Use crimping pliers to secure the wire, tucking it with the notch at the pliers' tip.

**6** a Slip the bead over the wire and tie a knot next to the bead. Trim the excess cord.

b Repeat steps 4–6a for the remaining cords.

## tips

• For beads with a smaller diameter, fold a 4-in. (10 cm) piece of flexible beading wire and use it as a needle to thread the cord through each bead.

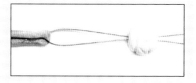

• If your beads have extra-large holes, tie an additional knot on top of the first to prevent them from slipping.

# String
## unpretentious
## pearls

**Silk cord proves the perfect
companion for a casual look**

**designed by Irina Miech**

"Finally, I'm able to string pearls on something other than beading wire. What more could a pearl-loving girl ask for?"

The muted shades of these silk ribbons pair splendidly with pearls in a low-key lariat. Look for pearls with a 2 mm or larger hole; they'll accommodate the ribbons.

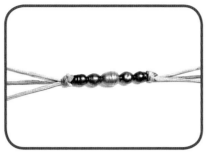

**1** lariat • Over three ribbons, center five pearls. On each side, with all three ribbons, tie an overhand knot (Basics, p. 6) next to the end pearl.

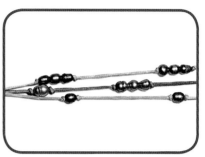

**2** On each end of each ribbon, tie an overhand knot 1–3 in. (2.5–7.6 cm) from the previous knot. String one to three pearls and tie an overhand knot. Repeat.

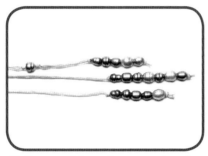

**3** On one ribbon, tie an overhand knot 5–6 in. (13–15 cm) from each end. String a pearl and tie an overhand knot. Approximately 3 in. (7.6 cm) from each end of each ribbon, tie an overhand knot. String five to seven pearls and tie an overhand knot. Trim the excess ribbon.

## Materials

**lariat 35 in. (89 cm)**
- **65–75** 8–12 mm large-hole pearls, in four or five colors
- **3** 42-in. (1.1 m) silk ribbons, in three colors
- diagonal wire cutters

**earrings**
- **12** 8–12 mm large-hole pearls
- 42-in. (1.1 m) silk ribbon
- pair of earring wires
- chainnose and roundnose pliers, or **2** pairs of chainnose pliers
- diagonal wire cutters

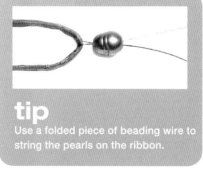

**tip**
Use a folded piece of beading wire to string the pearls on the ribbon.

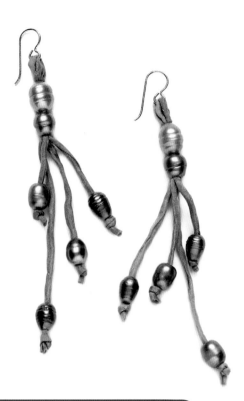

**1** earrings • Cut two 5-in. (13 cm) pieces of ribbon. Fold them both in half. String two pearls over the fold (Tip, p. 37), leaving a loop above the pearls.

**2** On each end, string a pearl. Tie an overhand knot (Basics) on each end of each ribbon, staggering the placement of the knots. Trim the excess ribbon.

**3** Open the loop of an earring wire (Basics) and attach the dangle. Make a second earring to match the first.

**66** I am most inspired by nature, and whenever possible use organic and natural materials in my designs. **99**

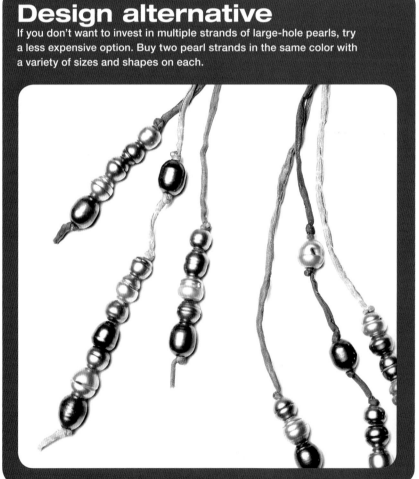

# Design alternative

If you don't want to invest in multiple strands of large-hole pearls, try a less expensive option. Buy two pearl strands in the same color with a variety of sizes and shapes on each.

# Crystals add
# spark
# to silk

# Shimmering dangles contrast with this necklace's soft macramé cord

## designed by Monica Lueder

It takes opposing elements to pull this necklace together. Silk cord adds a soft twist of matte color that won't overpower the subtle shimmer of faceted beads. Likewise, the organic variation in the knots balances the symmetry of the cut crystals. This attraction of opposites will guarantee a dynamic look for any occasion.

1 String a faceted bead on a 2-in. (5cm) head pin and make a wrapped loop (Basics, p. 7). Make 18 to 32 bead units.

2 To knot the silk cords: Bring the left cord over and around the right cord and then over itself. Tighten the knot. Bring the right cord over and around the left and then over itself. Tighten the knot. Continue knotting with alternating cords until the strand is within 1 in. (2.5cm) of the desired length. (My necklaces are 14½ in./36.8cm.)

3 Open a jump ring (Basics) and attach a bead unit to a knotted loop at the center of the necklace. Close the jump ring.

4 On each side, attach bead units to the cord at ½-in. (1.3cm) intervals. Check the fit, allowing 1 in. (2.5cm) for finishing on each end. Add or untie knots, if necessary.

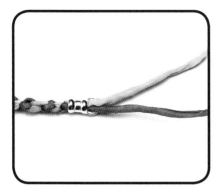  

**5** On each side, tie the ends together in an overhand knot (Basics). Apply glue to the knot, and string a crimp end so the knot is centered within it.

**6** On each end, trim the cords close to the crimp end. Flatten the center section of the crimp end with chainnose pliers.

**7** Open a jump ring and attach an S-hook clasp and one of the crimp ends. Close the jump ring. Repeat on the other end, substituting a soldered jump ring for the clasp.

## Materials

- ◆ **18–32** faceted rectangular beads
- ◆ **2** 18–22-in. (46–56cm) silk cords, in two colors
- ◆ **18–32** 2-in. (5cm) head pins
- ◆ **20–34** 6mm inside diameter (ID) jump rings
- ◆ **2** 5mm crimp ends
- ◆ S-hook clasp and 6mm ID soldered jump ring
- ◆ chainnose and roundnose pliers
- ◆ diagonal wire cutters
- ◆ E6000 adhesive

## design guidelines

• To add more color, braid three strands of cord.

• If you use soldered jump rings, string the bead units as you make the knots. When making the dangles, make the first half of a wrapped loop. Attach the jump ring and then complete the wraps.

# Knotted leather cord and beads team up in a versatile choker

### designed by
### Miachelle DePiano

Dress up leather cord with large beads and a glass pendant in this fast and easy choker. Using just two knots – the square and the overhand – even those who have never done macramé can complete this piece with confidence. The zigzagging knotwork provides a chic setting that can go dressy or casual, and an asymmetrical finish lends a playful attitude.

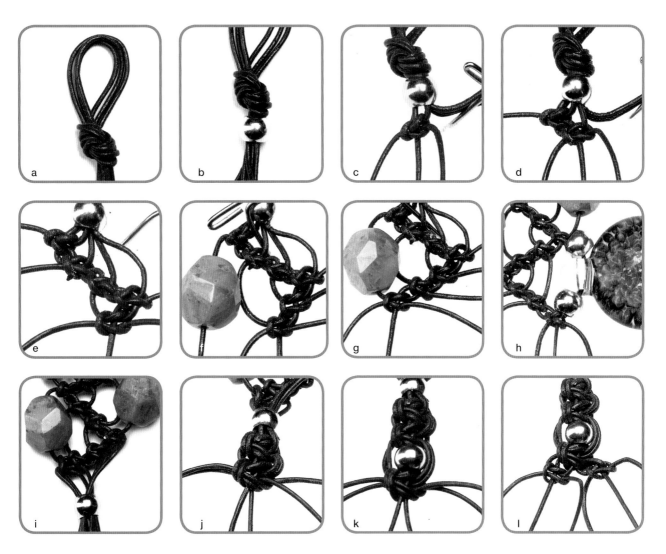

1 Cut the leather cord into three 3-yd. (2.7m) lengths. Gather them so the ends are even with each other, and fold them in half. Make an overhand knot (Basics, p. 6) near the fold, leaving an opening large enough for the tip of your index finger to fit through (photo a).

2 String a 6mm bead over all six cords (photo b).

3 Pin the knot to the macramé board, and spread out the cords. Number them 1–6 from left to right. Make a square knot (figures 1 and 2) around cord 2 with cords 1 and 3 (photo c).

4 Renumber the cords 1–6. Make a square knot around cord 3 with cords 2 and 4 (photo d).

5 Repeat across, each time setting aside the left-hand cord, picking up the next cord on the right, and making a square knot around the middle cord of the three-cord group.

6 After you've made a knot with cords 4 and 6, work the pattern in reverse. Begin by making a square knot with cords 5 and 3 (photo e). Continue tying knots to the left. Before making the knot with cords 3 and 1, string a 14mm bead (photo f).

7 Tie the knot (photo g), and work the pattern to the right. Again, before knotting with the final three cords, string a 14mm.

8 Continue working this pattern until you're preparing to string the 12th bead. Instead of stringing a

14mm, string a 6mm, the pendant, and a 6mm. Tie the knot as usual (photo h).

9 Continue working the pattern until you've strung 22 14mms. String a 6mm over all six strands (photo i).

10 Tie two square knots, using cords 1 and 2 and 5 and 6 to knot around cords 3 and 4 (photo j).

11 String a 6mm over the two middle strands, and tie a square knot after it as in step 10 (photo k).

12 Separate the cords into two groups of three. Make a square knot around cord 2 with cords 1 and 3 and around cord 5 with cords 4 and 6 (photo l).

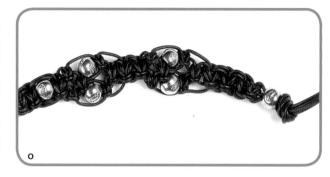

**13** Tie a square knot around cords 3 and 4 with cords 2 and 5 (**photo m**).

**14** String a 6mm on cord 2, and tie a square knot with cords 1 and 3. String a 6mm on cord 5, and tie a square knot with cords 4 and 6 (**photo n**).

**15** Repeat step 13.

**16** Repeat step 10.

**17** Repeat steps 12–14.

**18** Repeat step 13.

**19** Tie three square knots, using cords 1 and 2 and 5 and 6 to knot around cords 3 and 4. Test for fit. Make more or fewer knots as needed.

**20** String a 6mm, and tie an overhand knot against it. Slip the knot through the loop you made in step 1 to make sure it won't slip out. If it's too small, make another knot over the first. Test again, and make any necessary adjustments. Trim the cords evenly about ¼ in. (6mm) after the knot. **Photo o** shows this end of the necklace.

## Materials

**necklace 14½ in. (36.8cm)**

- glass pendant
- **22** 14mm beads
- **10** 6mm large-hole beads (holes must be able to accommodate six strands of 1mm leather cord)
- 9 yd. (8.2m) 1mm leather cord
- macramé board or self-healing
- Styrofoam pad
- T-pins

## tip

Leather cord can be as much as 25 percent thicker than its labeled diameter. Try to find cord that is as close to 1mm as possible, as using cord that is even a bit thicker will alter your results. Furthermore, leather cord is relatively weak and is easier to break or tear than you may expect. If, as you're knotting, you see a crack forming in your cord, grasp the cord above the crack, and proceed. As long as you're careful, you should be able to get past the crack without breaking the cord. The structure of the macramé should support the cracked cord and prevent further damage.

## macramé square knot

**1** Cross the right-hand cord over the core and the left-hand cord under the core. This creates a loop between each cord and the core. Pass the right-hand cord through the loop on the left from front to back and the left-hand cord through the other loop from back to front (**figure 1**).

**2** Cross the left-hand cord over and the right-hand cord under the core. Pass the cords through the loops (**figure 2**), and tighten.

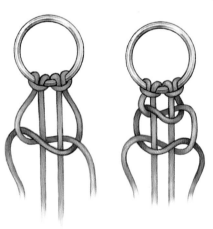

**figure 1**          **figure 2**

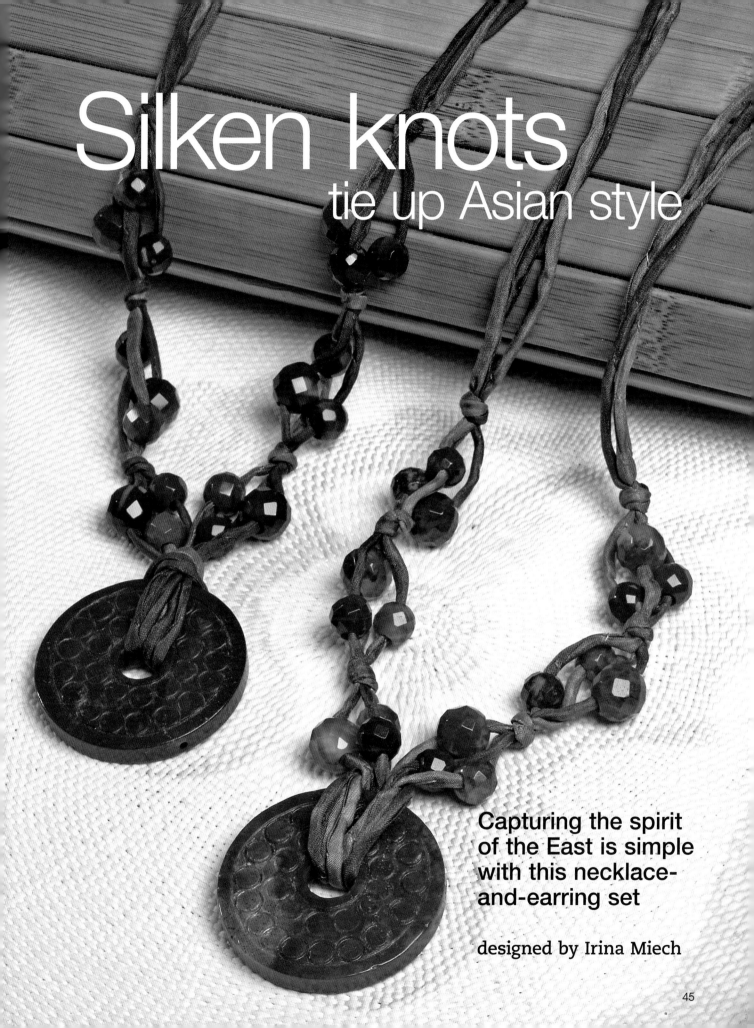

# Silken knots
## tie up Asian style

**Capturing the spirit
of the East is simple
with this necklace-
and-earring set**

designed by Irina Miech

A delicately engraved donut and knotted silk ribbons form the basis of a subtle, exotic jewelry set. Try different color choices to change the mood.

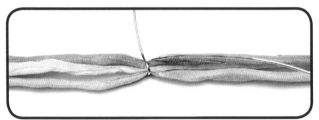

**1** necklace • Fold three silk ribbons in half and string the ends through a donut pendant. Pull the ribbons through the resulting loop.

**2** On each side of the pendant, string a large-hole bead on each ribbon. Tie an overhand knot (Basics, p. 6) with all three ribbons. Repeat the pattern twice.

**3** Determine the finished length of your necklace. (Mine is 17 in./43cm.)
Cut a 4-in. (10cm) piece of 22-gauge wire. Make the first half of a wrapped loop (Basics). String one set of ribbons through the loop, positioning the loop within 2 in. (5cm) of the desired finished length. Repeat on the other side.

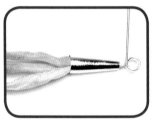

**4** On each side, tightly wrap the wire tail around the ribbons. Trim the ribbons 1/4 in. (6mm) from the wraps and apply Dritz Fray Check to the ends.

**5** On each end, string a cone over the wire stem and make the first half of a wrapped loop.

**6** On a head pin, string a 5mm bead. Make the first half of a wrapped loop.
Attach a 2-in. (5cm) chain and complete the wraps.

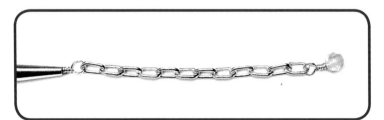

**7** On one end, string the chain extender and complete the wraps. Repeat on the other end, substituting an S-hook clasp for the chain extender.

## Materials

**necklace**

- 4mm engraved donut pendant
- **18** 8–10mm large-hole, faceted round beads
- 5mm round bead
- 8 in. (20cm) 22-gauge half-hard wire
- **3** 18–22-in. (46–56cm) silk ribbons
- 2 in. (5cm) chain, 4–5mm links
- 1½-in. (3.8cm) head pin
- **2** 12mm cones
- S-hook clasp
- chainnose and roundnose pliers
- diagonal wire cutters
- Dritz Fray Check

**earrings**

- **2** 10mm large-hole,
- faceted round beads
- 6 in. (15cm) 24-gauge half-hard wire
- 7 in. (18cm) silk ribbon
- **2** 12mm cones
- pair of earring wires
- chainnose and roundnose pliers
- diagonal wire cutters
- Dritz Fray Check

## tip

Consider using large-hole silver spacers instead of faceted beads for greater visual contrast.

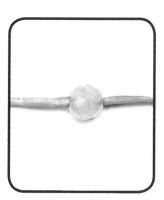

1 earrings • Cut a 3½-in. (8.9cm) piece of silk ribbon. Center a bead on the ribbon.

2 Cut a 3-in. (7.6cm) piece of 22-gauge wire. Make the first half of a wrapped loop (Basics). String the ribbon ends through the loop. Tightly wrap the wire tail around the ribbons. Trim the ends 1/8 in. (3mm) from the wraps and apply Dritz Fray Check to the ends.

3 String a cone on the wire. Make a wrapped loop.

4 Open the loop of an earring wire (Basics). Attach the dangle and close the loop. Make a second earring to match the first.

# CONTRIBUTORS

**Ashley Bunting** loves working with new products, especially fibers. Her latest book from Kalmbach Publishing is titled Fiber and Cord Jewelry. Contact Ashley at missashleykate@gmail.com or visit missashleykate.com.

Contact **Kelly Conedera** at kelly@xogallery.comor visit xogallery.com.

Contact **Miachelle DePiano** at cosmoaccessories@cox.net or visit cosmopolitanaccessories.net.

**Lorelei Eurto** is a self-proclaimed "girl with a passion for beads." She's been creating beaded jewelry since 2007. Contact Lorelei at ljeurto@gmail.com or visit loreleieurtojewelry.com.

Contact **Linda Jones** via her Web site, wirejewellery.co.uk.

**Jane Konkel** is a former associate editor of Bead Style magazine. Contact her in care of Kalmbach Books.

**Monica Lueder** loves working crystals into her jewelry designs and is always experimenting with different looks. Contact Monica at mdesign@wi.rr.com.

Contact **Michelle Mach** at beadgirl@fiatslug.com or visit michellemach.com.

**Irina Miech** is an artist, teacher, and the author of 10 books on jewelry design. She also oversees her two retail bead supply stores, Eclectica and The Bead Studio, in Brookfield, Wis., where she teaches classes. Contact Irina at Eclectica, 262-641-0910, or via email at eclecticainfo@sbcglobal.net.

Contact **Linda Osterhoudt** at lindaoohlinda@earthlink.net or visit ohlinda.com.

**Ayla Phillips Pizzo** fell in love with beads after randomly picking up a beading kit to break the boredom of an Illinois winter. She now owns Ayla's Originals in Evanston, Illinois, and her Ayla's Own Jewelry line has received national attention. Contact her at info@aylasorignals.com, or visit www.aylasorignals.com.